19,953

301.45 Griffin, John
G 87t   Howard

A time to be human

301.45 Griffin, John
G87t   Howard   19,953

A time to be human

6.95

DATE	BORROWER'S NAME	
SEP 30 '82	*Mancelo Valdz Lutz*	

301.45   19,953
G87t   Griffin, John Howard

A time to be human.

© THE BAKER & TAYLOR CO.

A TIME
TO BE
HUMAN

John Howard Griffin

A TIME
TO BE
HUMAN

MACMILLAN PUBLISHING CO., INC.
New York
COLLIER MACMILLAN PUBLISHERS
London

PICTURE CREDITS: Culver Pictures, 70–71; Bruce Davidson (Magnum), 23; Ben Fernandez (Black Star), 92; Gregory Griffin, 40; John Howard Griffin, 97; Hella Hammid (Photo Researchers), 33; Declan Haun (Black Star), 79; Danny Lyon (Magnum), 50, 87; Don Rutledge (courtesy of John Howard Griffin), 41–43; Wide World Photos, 8; YIVO Institute for Jewish Research, 14–15.

Macmillan Publishing Co., Inc.
866 Third Avenue, New York, N.Y. 10022
Collier Macmillan Canada, Ltd.

Printed in the United States of America
10 9 8 7 6 5 4 3 2

LIBRARY OF CONGRESS CATALOGING IN PUBLICATION DATA

Griffin, John Howard, date
    A time to be human.

    SUMMARY: One man's account of prejudice and racism in the United States.
    1. Griffin, John Howard, date —Juvenile literature.   2. Texas—Biography—Juvenile literature.   3. United States—Race question—Juvenile literature.   4. Afro-Americans—Civil rights—Juvenile literature.   [1. Griffin, John Howard, date   2. Race problems.   3. Afro-Americans—Civil rights]   I. Title.
E185.98G74A33   301.45′1   76–47468
ISBN 0–02–737200–4

For Roland Hayes

JOHN HOWARD GRIFFIN

Born in Dallas and raised in Ft. Worth, Texas, John Howard Griffin attended high school and college in France, where he prepared for a career in medicine and psychiatry. Active in the U.S. Air Force in the South Pacific during World War II, he was twice wounded, resulting in the loss of most of his sight.

He returned to France at the end of the war, nearly blind, and began working in music and musicology, including private studies with Nadia Boulanger and Robert Casadesus and graduate research in Medieval Music and Gregorian Chant at the Benedictine Abbey of Solesmes. At the same time, he also began studies in philosophy, later continued under the direction of Jacques Maritain.

In 1947, completely blind, Mr. Griffin returned to the United States to attend schools for the blind and began lecturing on musicology. Later, he turned to a career as a writer. His first novel, *The Devil Rides Outside*, was published in 1952 and it was followed by three more novels and numerous magazine articles.

In 1957, his sight was partially restored after extensive medical treatment. During the next several years, he was commissioned by the University of Texas, the B'nai B'rith, and other organizations to do sociological studies on racism. It was one of these studies which led him to the experiment he reported in his book *Black Like Me*.

In the years following the publication of that book,

Mr. Griffin has worked with community leaders to open up communication between the races in cities like Los Angeles, Detroit, Cleveland, St. Louis, Wichita and others. He has also lectured on prejudice and racism at many universities, colleges, high schools and grade schools throughout the United States and extensively in Canada, France and Belgium. Recently he completed a series of seven documentaries on racial prejudice for Canadian radio and television and the National Public Radio network in the United States. He has also produced approximately twenty similar documentaries for French National Television.

When men do not get twisted and maimed beyond recognition, when they are allowed to live—the purpose of government is achieved. . . . From the time of the Three Dynasties men have been running in all directions. How can they find time to be human?

Thomas Merton, *The Way of Chuang Tzu*

PREFACE

My first vivid memory in life begins with the word "nigger." As a very small child I used that word in speaking to a black man in my grandfather's grocery store in south Dallas. I had scarcely spoken when I was jolted by a hard slap across my face and by the anger in my grandfather's voice as he snapped, "They're people—don't you ever let me hear you call them niggers again."

In preparing this book, the memory of that incident emerged fresh again. But it could just as well have happened yesterday or this morning because the world is still full of children who learn contemptuous terms for other people, and who use them and who go on being formed by them.

This is a personal book. I do not represent myself as a spokesman for black people or for anyone else. I will simply talk about my own experiences with racism: first, as a white child growing up in Texas, then for seven weeks as a black man in the South in 1959, and since then as a white man once again in the ghettos of most of our major cities and in many other countries.

Many people believe that racism and prejudice are things of the past in this country, that civil rights legislation and greater enlightenment have conquered discrimination.

It is true that things have changed in the past ten or fifteen years. Blacks and other minority people can eat and find accommodations pretty much wherever they want now, and most can vote. But it is also true that racism is still rampant both in this country and around the world. Many cities are in turmoil, resisting any attempts to achieve equality in education through busing. And there is still much discrimination in employment, housing and equal justice under the law. In some cities, tests have been made. A well-dressed black lady with perfect credentials will look for apartments in better-class apartment houses. Often she will be told that every unit is taken, that nothing is available, that those empty apartments have just been rented. An hour later an equally well-dressed white lady, with essentially the same credentials, will follow in her footsteps and find apartments everywhere. Such experiments have recently been reported in *The New York Times*.

But most newspapers do not talk much about such incidents now. Racism is no longer "news," and therefore many of us live with an illusion that all the problems have been solved and that we enjoy racial harmony in this land.

But the minority press does carry full coverage of racial injustices and minority people are deeply aware of the crippling extent of racism in their own lives and elsewhere. As a result we have continued to be essentially two groups of citizens—the black minority and the white majority—with two entirely different sets of information about life in this country. The deepest shock I experienced as a black man was the realization that *everything* is utterly different when one is the victim of racial prejudice.

To my mind this country is involved in profound

tragedy. The problems of racism have not been solved and they will never be solved until we can learn to communicate with one another. Yet we have never listened to the words of minority spokesmen who have told us truths about ourselves and our country. As in the past, if a minority person tells us truths about ourselves that offend our prejudices, we promptly brand that person "arrogant" or "uppity" and try to get rid of him.

After my experiment as a black man in the Deep South, part of my work involved going into cities all over this land to set up communications between black and white leaders. Often I found myself in situations where I sat at conference tables with blacks and whites who wanted to solve the problems within their local communities. I knew, and every black person seated there knew, that any of them could tell the whites the truth about prejudice and injustice at the local level far better than I possibly could. But because I was white once again, I could tell the truth without antagonizing the whites. If a black person said exactly the same words, no matter how tactfully he or she might put it, white leaders would be offended and the attempt at communication would turn into anger, with whites referring to blacks as arrogant or smart-alecky or rude.

Whites always think that such misunderstandings occur somewhere else. They cannot really believe that black people in Wichita, Kansas, or Oakland, California, felt the same resentments and frustrations as black people in the Deep South. They also cannot believe that they carry prejudices as deep as those of white Southerners.

I remember I was once called in to give a talk on racism in a small town in Pennsylvania. This town had no black residents, although a black industrial psychologist held a position there. The problem there, they said, was not racism but friction between Protestants and Catholics. A professor at one of the local colleges got Protestants and Catholics together to sponsor my lecture. The house was crowded. I spoke frankly about the way in which people who are persuaded they are not prejudiced, who do not *want* to be prejudiced, can be tainted with racism without ever perceiving it. I talked of the difficulty most people have in listening to truths from black people without becoming offended, whereas they would applaud those same truths coming from a white person.

In that sea of white faces, I watched the black industrial psychologist's face. He smiled and gave a slow nod of agreement.

Afterward at a reception for those who had helped sponsor the lecture, the professor was jubilant. He said it was the first time local Protestants and Catholics had got together on any project, and that it had been a glorious success. Turning to the black psychologist, he said, "Don't you view this night as a turning point in the history of our community?"

"Well, I'm not too sure about that," the black man said.

"What do you mean?" the professor asked quickly.

"I mean that I'm the only black man in this community. I have a fine job and am paid a good salary. Everyone seems to be glad I am working here. But so long as I have to house my wife and children in a town twenty miles away because no one in this community will rent or sell me a house, then don't expect me to get excited about your 'historic turning points,' " the psychologist said calmly.

The professor flared with anger. I heard a minister mutter, "I knew it was going to mean trouble inviting that black man here tonight."

The professor almost shouted, "Well, I'll tell you one thing. If you have that kind of attitude, I don't know how you can expect us to do anything for you."

The psychologist would not back down. He held to his point, angering more and more whites even though he never raised his voice or spoke rudely. I saw that a crisis was near, that tempers were getting out of hand, and I said, "This is very interesting. When I talked about the same sort of thing earlier this evening, none of you thought it really applied to this community. You thought I was talking about other people in other parts of the country. Now this man is telling you exactly the same kind of truths I discussed earlier. You gave me a standing ovation; you are furious with him for saying the same things."

It was a cold slap. The professor who had been in such a fury immediately saw the point. He apologized for his bad behavior and thanked the psychologist for helping him to see his own prejudice.

So this has always been, and remains, a great problem, even with the sincerest men. Exactly the same thing holds when Chicanos and Native American Indians try to make people understand their problems.

What I want to do is place before you as much information about racism as I can in a few pages, in the hope that some of it may be clarifying and maybe we can understand how we have arrived where we are today. I believe that only through deeper awareness and understanding can we hope to cure the wounds that racism causes in ourselves as well as in those whom we hurt through our prejudices. Perhaps if enough people become aware we will decide that we don't want this kind of racism and prejudice anymore.

ONE

It is clear that racism and racial prejudice exist every-where. No country is spared—it ranges from the black racism of Uganda to the white racism of South Africa and Rhodesia. Racism festers between Protestants and Catholics in Ireland, between Muslims and Christians in Lebanon, between Arab and Israeli peoples in the Middle East, between French- and English-speaking Canadians, between the Flemish and the Walloons of Belgium.

How did we get that way? Why do we who think of ourselves as good, kind, decent human beings allow racism to continue among us when it not only destroys the victims but also, if we could only see it, destroys us.

I am going to write for a moment about the South, not because the South is more racist than any other corner of this land but because that is where I was born, in Texas, and where I had my early formation. Also, the patterns that formed us in prejudice are a little clearer and easier to understand in the South. But basic patterns are the same everywhere, even though they may appear to differ.

Many of us in the South had a formation that built racial prejudice in us and at the same time persuaded us that we were not prejudiced. Often we were taught to look down on the viciously prejudiced, to view them as "white trash." Great numbers of us had the kind of experiences that turned us into racists without our ever understanding what was happening to us.

As small children many of us had the experience of frequent and close contact with black people. We were allowed to play quite freely with black children. We were often reared with the help of a black lady. You did not have to be rich to have black help in those days. Our early years were often surrounded by the love of black people—the lady who helped care for us, the children we had as playmates.

But when we were still very young, perhaps six or seven, society, in the kind and gentle voices of our parents, grandparents, aunts and uncles, did a terrible thing to us. Society told us that the time had come when we must stop playing with black children. We were made to understand that we had to change, in subtle ways, our attitudes toward the black lady who helped care for us. I remember my Georgia grandmother, for example, telling me that I was getting too big to sit on that black lady's lap.

Society explained to us that black people preferred it that way, that it would embarrass them if we did not change our behavior and draw away from them. These explanations, filled with racist myths, led us to conclude that black people were somehow "different" from us in their human needs and desires, that they were not frustrated by things that would frustrate whites.

So we were allowed to learn to love black people and then we were taught in a sense to stop loving. "They're just not like us," everyone explained. But this was done so gently that we grew up with the illusion that we continued to love those whom we patronizingly called "our Negroes." We saw them as "other" and "different" and "not like us"—and always that implied that they were somehow inferior to us.

Our distress over many of the cruelties blacks suffered at the hands of white people only strengthened our belief that we were not prejudiced. I recall an incident when I was seven. Whites lynched a black man in a town ninety miles from where we lived. This lynching was given wide publicity. They even postponed it for three days so they could bring in special tourist trains for people who wanted to see it. Two thousand tourists—men, women and children—flocked into that town of Waco, Texas.

According to contemporary newspaper accounts, the lynching took the form of burning the young man at the stake. Parents held their children above the crowd so the children could see what was going on.

But great numbers of us did not go. We sat at home hearing our parents and grandparents cry in anguish against such monstrousness. How could "civilized people" in this century burn a fellow human being at the stake, no matter what he might have done? they asked. How could parents take children to view such a thing? A few days later we watched their sadness when it was revealed that the mob had lynched an innocent man.

Such incidents persuaded many of us that we were not "like that." We detested the "trash" who did things like that. We detested their prejudice, and this led us to believe that we had no prejudice.

All of these early learned behavior patterns went deep in us. In denying our own prejudices, we still thought racism was "human nature," which it is not at all. What we failed to realize is simply this: when children are formed in an atmosphere that permits the suppression of fellow human beings, it ends up tainting us in ways we never dream. Surely few crimes are more tragic than the crime of fostering in children a false view of what man is by teaching them to believe that any other humans are basically different in their human needs or in their response to the frustration of those needs. This concept of fellow human beings as "other" is at the base of all racism.

Similar patterns hold true everywhere. In Nazi Germany the non-Jewish child was brought up to view Jewish people as "other." In Ireland today the Protestant child is taught to believe that the Catholic child is "other," and the Catholic child is taught to see the Protestant child as "other." We find the same pattern when we hear people refer to the French as "immoral" or to Mexicans as "lazy," or to any group as possessing "racial characteristics" of a degrading nature. And once we believe that a group of people is "different" then we can believe that they do not need or deserve the same rights and liberties we always claim for ourselves.

Many of us go through life without ever realizing how deeply tainted we are by these prejudices. When we do realize it, someone has usually had to point it out to us.

Such an event occurred to me when I was sent to school in France in my teens. I attended a *lycée* where we had a few black students. As a person who thought himself without prejudice, I was delighted to have black people in my classes. It was the first time I had ever experienced such a thing.

And yet the first time I went out to a public eating place with a fellow white student, when one of those same black schoolmates I had been so pleased to have in class came in and took a table across the room, I reacted according to the old patterns I had learned in the South. I pushed my chair back from the table and asked in an offended voice, "Do you allow *them* to eat in the same restaurant with us?"

"Why not?" my schoolmate asked bluntly.

Why not? I realized with a sick feeling that I had grown into my teens without ever hearing anyone ask that question. Even worse, I felt astonished that I had never even thought to ask it myself. I had simply accepted the "customs" of my region which said that black people could not eat in the same room with us, or drink from the same water fountain, or even use the same toilet. Why couldn't they? It had never occurred to me to ask. Only then did I realize how deeply I was prejudiced and how that prejudice deformed my thinking about other human beings.

Still, if anyone had suggested that we practiced racism in America I would have denied it with all my heart. During those years in France I witnessed the rise of Adolph Hitler and Nazism in neighboring Germany. To me that was racism. I thought racism concerned only the Nazi suppression of Jewish people, and because the victims were Jewish I made no connection between the racism that murdered the Jews of Europe and the racism that afflicted minority people in the U.S. I heard the Nazis say the same things about Jewish people that I had grown up hearing about black people in the U.S., but I did not recognize the similarities.

When World War II came, in 1939, all Americans were ordered to return to the U.S. Since France was a country that had helped to form me, I could not see deserting my friends there in this time of great trouble. I remained in Tours and soon became involved in the underground and resistance movements. In those early days of the war, most of our efforts were concentrated on trying to save German-Jewish people from the Nazis. Teams smuggled Jewish families across the border into France and turned them over to other teams who guided them to the city of Tours. There we hid them in cheap back-street boarding-houses until we could arrange transportation to take them to the port of St. Nazaire where other teams arranged to get them to England.

We had some success at the outset. But when Nazi armies began to invade France, new government regulations required that we carry identification and safe-conduct papers. These papers were checked every two or three blocks. In those early days of our work, we were unskilled. We had no way of getting papers for the Jewish families we were hiding and so could not move them to safety.

One night an event occurred that gave me my first clear insight into the basic reality of racism. That night I had the terrible task of going into those rooms in the boarding-houses where we had hidden our Jewish guests to tell them we were not going to succeed. We had moved them that far toward freedom, but the German armies were catching up with us and we had no way to move them any further.

When I went into those rooms that night the parents guessed why I had come even before I spoke. They said they knew it was over for them, that as soon as the Nazis moved in they would be rounded up and shipped back

to Germany and the concentration camps. Then they did something that shocked me. They asked me to take their children away from them, because we could move children under the age of fifteen without any papers.

I realized then that I was in the presence of terrible human tragedy—the tragedy of parents who loved their children, who had little hope that they would ever see them again, who were giving their children away to a virtual stranger so that at least the children would escape the concentration camps and the gas chambers. The full force of this tragedy was there in all its reality in those rooms.

Suddenly all of our endless conversations about racism as university students seemed empty and meaningless. Racism, with the rise of Hitler, had been an obsessive topic of conversation among students, the great intellectual preoccupation. But sitting in those rooms with men and women and children, innocent of any crime, pursued only because they were born Jewish, made me realize that we had never understood anything about the true evils of a racist system that solved problems by murdering those men, women and children.

Everything became clear: the smallness of those cheap rooms, the brightly flowered wallpaper, the living, breathing human beings whose lives no one would now be able to save. And I knew then that I could walk out into the streets and meet people who considered themselves perfectly decent, who had no knowledge of what was going on inside those rooms and who would go on rationalizing and justifying the very racism that led to the tragedy in those rooms.

Sometimes in discussing racism with people, I wish I could simply take them into such rooms in this country. I think of rooms where I have sat with heartbroken human beings who happen to be black and who have suffered great tragedy for no other reason. I think of a room in a farmhouse near Hattiesburg, Mississippi, where I sat with the mother of Clyde Kennard.

Clyde Kennard was a gifted young black American who served in the Army, first in Germany in World War II and then in Korea. He fought to defend the rights and liberties which we call "American." When he returned to his homeland, he attended the University of Chicago for three years. When his stepfather died of a stroke, Kennard went back to his home in Mississippi to take care of his mother and to run the farm. In 1960, he applied for admission to finish his schooling at Mississippi Southern University in Hattiesburg. The only objection to his admission was his color yet everything was done to stop him. He persisted, saying he had the right to attend a public university and that if he did not insist on his rights he would be betraying the children he hoped someday to have. When he would not back down, he was jailed on trumped-up charges and allowed to die of untreated cancer in what amounted to a deliberate, slow lynching.

Sitting in Clyde Kennard's house, looking into the grief-stricken face of a mother whose son had suffered martyrdom, I knew that the scene was no different from the scenes in those rooms in Tours and that the same conditions held. I knew that here, too, I could go outside of that room and find people who considered themselves decent human beings, and who—knowing nothing of the reality within that room—went right on rationalizing and justifying the racism that led directly to the tragedy within that room.

The list of rooms could go on and on, and they are not only rooms in the South. Similar scenes occur in rooms in the ghettos of every major city in this land. I think, for example, of rooms in the ghetto of St. Louis where I have sat and listened to the despair of parents who say, "What can we do? We can't keep the children locked up in these two or three rooms. But the good influence we try to have on our children is wiped out the moment we let them go out and play in an area where six thousand people are crammed together in conditions of poverty, anger and despair."

No, racists have not lynched or shot or beaten these young people to death. But racism has fostered the system that every day murders them psychologically, spiritually and intellectually.

Black people everywhere, even those who have never suffered such discrimination, know about such things. The black press has carried this information so often ignored by the white press. Black people view the situation from the "inside." White people who never go inside those rooms always view it from the "outside" and wonder why black people feel such deep rage. We whites have no idea what racism really does to people.

When I returned to the U.S. after World War II, I lived in the South. There I began to hear the racist rationalizations I had heard all my life, but now they took on an ominously familiar sound.

How often we heard talk about "our race problem" and

"our Negro problem," just as the Nazis had talked about their "Jewish problem." And today we talk about "our Indian problem." It is clear that these are not "Negro problems" or "Jewish problems" or "Indian problems," but problems of racism.

Since we had seen where racism led in Europe, I began to wonder if we were not headed in the same direction in America. I began to do studies dealing with the problems of racism, regardless of who the victim group might be. One of the striking realizations that came from such studies was simply this: the patterns of racism are identical regardless of where or when they occur and regardless of who victimizes whom.

Racism always involves an injustice committed by one person or group against another person or group for reasons of race, color, religion or political ideology. It is fatal in the end because it always works to damage *both* groups. The more racism succeeds, the more it damages both the racist and his victims.

Often since that night in Tours, France, I have thought of a statement that I learned in my youth. It was Edmund Burke's "I know of no way of drawing up an indictment against a whole people."

It seems to me that this is the key to the racist fallacy. The Nazis had drawn up an indictment against the entire Jewish community. Once that indictment had been drawn —and far more important, once men consented to it and did not immediately cry "No!"—the rest followed.

In 1959, after having dealt with the problems of racism for almost twenty years, I was asked to do a study dealing with the rise in the suicide-tendency rate among black people in the Deep South. This did not mean that black people were committing suicide directly. Rather it concerned a rise in violent incidents that were not connected, incidents in which blacks would appear to go berserk and lash out against whites, often strangers, for no apparent cause. The blacks would then make no attempt to escape and when caught would say something to the effect that they did not care if they lived or died.

What triggered the rise in such incidents? I was asked by a sociologist at the University of Texas to find out. I sent out questionnaires to Southern whites and to Southern blacks—to educators, business and professional people and community leaders.

The replies from whites all said pretty much the same thing. It was inevitable. We whites have always said the same things about black people. Almost everyone remarked that my study was "ridiculous," since it was racially characteristic of blacks that they never committed suicide. "They are just naturally a happy-go-lucky people," one said. Another wrote, "When something troubles a Negro, he goes out and finds himself a shady spot under a tree and sleeps it off." I am embarrassed even to repeat such things here, but this was said by people who sincerely believed it.

Two things were obvious in these replies from whites. First, I could not question the sincerity of these people. We have been brought up believing this myth about blacks. Second, it was evident that no matter how distinguished a person might be, or how much the vast majority accepted such myths, the myths are utterly untrue. The fact that a great many people agree to them does not make them true.

The history of suicides among black people and other minorities in this land is, and has always been, appalling. To suggest that black people, by racial characteristic, never commit suicide is simply to lie in the face of history and fact.

When the questionnaires came back from black people, I was astonished to note that not one contained any answers to my questions. The few that were returned were blank, but they were accompanied by explanatory letters. These said, in essence, "We don't answer this kind of questionnaire anymore. We have answered them in the past, but we will not answer them in the future." For the first time one of them used a term I had never heard before, but I found it accurate and illuminating. He said, "You probably can't help it, but you think *white*," as distinguished from thinking *human*. "We don't believe it's possible for a white man, even one trained in the sciences, to interpret his findings without thinking white and thereby falsifying the truth."

I realized they were fully justified in this. White people have taken perfectly reputable scientific data and interpreted it according to our white middle-class culture, to the detriment of truth. This has been, and still is, particularly true about IQ tests based on a purely white culture. Black children, long denied access to many aspects of that culture, rarely do well on such biased tests. People who think white will conclude that black children are therefore intellectually inferior to white children, which is false. In IQ tests based on black culture, black children excel over white children, but no one suggests that whites are therefore intellectually inferior.

Across two or three of those blank questionnaires, black people had written that the only way I could ever hope to understand anything about the plight of black people would be to wake up some morning in a black man's skin.

We have always heard this, and we have never believed it. But this challenge came so soon on my realization that we have never communicated that I began to wonder if I could really understand the problems of racism "from the outside."

And so I decided to try to arrange it so that I could, in fact, wake up some morning in a black man's skin.

There were other reasons for doing it, too. We knew quite a lot about racism. We knew, for example, that prejudice exists at the irrational level, placed in us as early learned behavior patterns. It is so deeply formed in us that many tend to view prejudice simply as part of human nature, which it is not at all. We also knew that we could no longer blame racial injustices on the "trash," as we had always done in the past. We knew that the world was full of people who are beautifully educated and who can handle reason superbly in every aspect of their existence except for a deeply held prejudice. When you approach people in this area of prejudice, their response tends to be immediate, emotional and irrational—and they seem impervious to scientific data. No, it isn't just the trash. We have people of great distinction who are racists —religious and professional leaders, judges, educators. I once did a study of Klan membership in an area of

Mississippi. Belonging to that Klan were two medical men, two judges, a sheriff, a constable, a bank president, two ministers, the owner and editor of the local newspaper.

So it seemed to me that if one of us could take on the "skin" of a black man, live whatever might happen and then share that experience with others, perhaps at the level of shared experience we might come to some understanding that was not possible at the level of pure reason.

People often ask me what was my motive, my "real motive," for doing this experiment in blackness. I think it finally boiled down to the fact that I had three children. I knew without any doubt that my own formation, no matter how benevolent, had filled me with prejudices at deep levels that had probably handicapped me for life. I might never see fellow human beings in their true light, simply as people. And I did not want my children, or the children of any person, white or black or any other color, to grow up in a climate of permissive suppression of fellow beings if I could do anything to prevent it. In other words, my deepest motive was simply to preserve my children and the children of others from the dehumanizing poison of racism.

In October of 1959 I went to New Orleans to undergo a series of medical treatments that would give me a pigment that would not wash off or wear off. During the time it took to transform me into a black man, I thought a great deal about the experiment. I felt my most important work would be to discover once and for all if we were really involved in racism in this land. We denied that we were. We claimed and sincerely believed in those days that in

America everyone was judged by his or her qualities as a human individual. I decided this was the important point to test.

In order to test this, I had to remain the same human individual. I decided to change nothing about myself except the color of my skin and to shave my head because of my straight hair. Otherwise, I would keep my name, keep my clothing, use my own credentials, and tell the truth in answer to any questions asked of me.

If we were not involved in the practice of racism then I would be judged by my qualities as a human individual and my life as a pigmented John Griffin would not differ drastically from the life I had always known as the white John Griffin. I was, after all, the same man, changed only in appearance. If, on the other hand, we were involved in looking on fellow human beings, seeing some visual mark like skin pigment, and consenting to draw up an indictment against a whole people (insofar as we consented to withhold from them rights which we guarantee equally to all people) then I would be included in that indictment and my life as a black John Griffin would differ in ways that I could not even imagine.

TWO

I had been sequestered in the home of an old friend while the medical change was taking place. Finally, one night around nine, I walked out of that house and into the streets of New Orleans, a well-dressed man with black skin. I did not have to wait long to find the answers to some of my questions. That first night brought great revelations which came simply from being black. I did not, however, realize the lasting significance of some of these events until years later.

I had not gone far before I encountered a middle-aged white man who looked at me curiously. I was apparently in a part of town where black men were not supposed to be at night. I asked him if he knew where I could find a room. He did not know but he was courteous and obviously took me for a black man who was new in the city. He suggested I look for a place on Dryades Street—the black ghetto. He did not show the slightest flicker of suspicion about my identity.

I then met two black men, one after the other, both middle-aged. I asked each of them the same question. Where could I find a room? They also handled me with courtesy, and they told me about two possible hotels in the black area.

To my amazement, neither of them showed the slightest hint of suspicion about my identity. This astonished me. I had never for one moment thought that I would pass as a black man to other black people. I had not even intended to try. In the first place, I did not think it would be possible for me to pass to black people, and I had thought that I would simply explain to them that I was a white man doing a sociological experiment. It was not important for me to pass to black people. My experiment involved white people and how they would treat me once they saw me as a black man.

The reasons why I thought I could not pass to black people, I realize today, are deeply significant. They have to do with "thinking white."

First, I did not think I could possibly pass because, although I had the skin color, I did not have the kind of bone structure or facial conformation or color of eyes that we think of as "Negroid." Yet I did not have to be in the black community, as a black man, for more than an hour to see what I had never before noticed as a white man. I saw black people with every type of bone structure, every type of facial conformation, and every density of pigment from so heavy it was black to so light it could not even be perceived. I saw black people with blue eyes, with green eyes, with gray eyes.

In a land where white men have abused black women sexually for so many years, the vast majority of black people in this country have white progenitors somewhere in their background. The pure African type is a rarity. Black people are deeply aware of this and, in almost every black home in which I have lived as a black man, they discussed quite freely and openly "where the white blood came from," which white man had abused whose mother or grandmother or great-grandmother.

But we do not see these realities. We think of blacks as looking a certain way. How often have we heard the expression, "They all look alike to me"? When we look at black people, we see them in stereotype. We now know that a deeply held prejudice will actually cause our senses to accommodate to the prejudice rather than to the reality of what they are seeing or hearing. Time and time again this has been demonstrated to me in my later experience.

I lectured once at the University of Washington. There I was introduced by a black anthropologist with the clearest gray eyes I have ever seen. Since she introduced me, the whole audience saw that she was black and that she had gray eyes. That night I did not discuss this matter of how the senses will accommodate to a deeply held prejudice rather than to reality. After my lecture I stood on the side of the stage talking with the anthropologist when a white woman came up to me and asked me if I would remove the colored glasses I was wearing. I removed them. She looked into my eyes and then asked, "How could you possibly have passed when you don't have black eyes?"

I immediately introduced her to the black anthropologist. She shook her hand. She looked into those clear gray eyes and she never caught on, because she turned back and waited for me to answer her question. She had just looked into the gray eyes of a black lady, but she still thought that all black people had black eyes. That is part of what black people mean about "thinking white."

The second reason I thought I could not possibly pass as a black man sprang from the same basic error of stereotyping people. I am embarrassed to admit it today, but I did not think I could pass because I did not know how to "speak Negro" or talk in what we think of as a "Negro dialect," and of course I didn't even try. We still have vast numbers of people in this land who think that unless you sound as though you were reading *Uncle Remus* you couldn't possibly sound like a black person. I have grown up hearing black people talk and yet it was not until I was black and living among blacks that I came to realize one hears just as many speech patterns among black people as one does among any other group of Americans. This was especially true in those days of rigid segregation when you might have been rubbing shoulders on one side with a black Ph.D. and on the other with someone scarcely able to read or write.

But here again, we go on "thinking white." We go on proving that a deeply held prejudice will cause our senses to accommodate to that prejudice. This is not a matter of education, but of perception. White college professors almost invariably ask me "What did you do about your voice, your dialect?"

This is one of the most crucial stumbling blocks in present-day relations between whites and blacks, and one of the reasons why communication is so frustrating. Black people constantly encounter whites, well-meaning and often educated whites, who simply view black people and hear black people in a totally unrealistic manner. This is called "selective inattention." It means that most of us, when we meet a black person, pay attention not to his looks and the words he pronounces but only to those things that *reinforce the stereotyped caricature we already hold of black people.*

So, I discovered immediately that I was going to pass to both whites and blacks, and this presented me with an ethical problem. Since segregation was total in those days, with few hotels for black people, I had to take rooms in the homes of black people whenever I traveled.

I would usually manage this by going into a community and asking the name of a local black minister who would know a great many people. I would ask him to recommend some family that might have a room I could occupy.

But I could not stay in the homes of black people under false pretenses, so I would try to tell my hosts the truth. I would say, "Before I can accept your shelter and the food from your table, I have to tell you a truth about myself that may surprise you." They would look at me expectantly and then I would announce, "I am not really a black man. I am a white man."

The looks of pain and distress in the eyes of my hosts told me clearly what they were too courteous to say in words. Their looks said, "Now I wonder what that preacher is doing saddling us with this big, black man who *thinks* he's white."

In all my experience, no one ever believed me except one man who had known me when I was white and whom I persuaded I was the same man. The others all thought I was suffering from some sort of delusion. Their eyes told them I was black, and they believed what they saw. Only later when the experiment received wide publicity did they believe that I had been telling them the truth all the time.

That first night in New Orleans brought other revelations. I found a tiny room in a ghetto hotel, a miserable room with no window, furnished with a bed and a cracked mirror on the wall. I sat on the bed, alone as a black man out in the world. I glanced at myself in the mirror and got two shocks. The first is not important. It was simply the shock of catching myself staring at a face in the mirror in which I could recognize nothing of myself.

The second shock, I realize now, was important and revealing. It was the shock of my involuntary reaction to that face in the mirror. I did not like that face. It was the face of a black man. It was somehow repulsive to me. I tried not to admit it. I tried to deny it. I was astounded to feel this involuntary movement of antipathy for that black man's face.

A sense of hopelessness and despair almost overwhelmed me, because I realized at that moment that although I had intellectually liberated myself from all of my prejudices, those prejudices had been so deeply ingrained that at the emotional level they were still very strong. I wondered how I could have committed myself so deeply to the cause of racial justice, only to discover now that at the level of emotional response I still carried those old racist poisons within me. I had to face this and recognize it for what it was.

Such a realization is immensely important today because we are finding people everywhere who do not want to be prejudiced, who argue against all racism, some of whom have even dedicated their lives to human justice without ever being liberated from those prejudices. Such people will say the right things and believe what they say, but if they have liberated their intelligence from their prejudices, they often have not liberated their emotions, and will reveal those prejudices to black people at the level of spontaneous emotional responses. Black people encounter this constantly. It is one of the reasons blacks say that "all whites are prejudiced." That statement may not be true, but if you are black, it seems to be true.

An important development stemming from this is that many of us equate our prejudices with guilt. And since we cannot admit our guilt, we cannot admit our prejudices, even to ourselves. Perhaps we must rethink this. I tell such people who come to me troubled by this sense of guilt that there is not necessarily any guilt attached to *having* the prejudices, since most of us are no more guilty of acquiring our prejudices than we are guilty of acquiring a disfiguring pockmark from some childhood illness. We got both when we were very young and before we could do anything to avoid them. But prejudice becomes a source of unspeakable guilt when we allow it to cloud our intelligence and to goad us into cooperating with unjust actions against other human beings.

Having recognized the depths of my own prejudices that I had carried with me since childhood, I was grateful to discover that within four or five days the old wounds were healed and all of the emotional repulsion was gone. It disappeared for the simple reason that I was staying in the homes of black families and I was experiencing at the emotional level, for the first time, what I had known intellectually for a long time. I was seeing that in families everything is the same for all people. This was revealed in simple and obvious ways. It was revealed in talk about what to have for supper and how to pay the bills; about which child should help with the dishes and which should help clear the table; about whether the child should do his homework when he got in from school or play for a while and then do his homework: about the things that all people in all families discuss. It was revealed in sitting with black parents and seeing that they responded to human frustration exactly as all other people do. The emotional garbage I had carried all of those years was dissolved in experiencing the fact that the "other" was not other at all. The other was my own self.

I saw then that there is no "other." All men face the same fundamental human problems of loving, of suffering, of fulfilling human aspirations and of dying. These are common denominators in all people of all cultures and all races and all ethnic categories. One of the truly tragic by-products of racism is that it leads some people to make it

more difficult for others to resolve these problems—and for no reason that makes any sense.

Jean Lacroix, the great French philosopher of communications has said that before we can authentically communicate with one another we must first "open ourselves to the other." I believe that before we can truly dialogue with one another we must perceive intellectually and then at the profoundest emotional level that there is no "other" —that the other is simply oneself in all the important essentials.

THREE

That first night in New Orleans also resolved all doubts about whether or not I was going to be judged as a human individual with my own qualities and faults and characteristics. I sat in that tiny cubicle of a hotel room and realized that I was in a city I had known well in the past. I had been there on concert tours and to autograph my earlier books. I had been put up in first-class hotels, received in the finest homes and entertained in famous restaurants.

But that night I sat alone in a part of town I had never known existed. I knew I was the same man with the same background, the same clothing, the same credentials, the same wallet. Everything about me was exactly the same except my color. And yet that night, for that one reason alone, because I was pigmented, I knew that all the money in the world could not buy me accommodations in any of those first-class hotels or restaurants that had received this same human individual as an honored guest before. And I knew that if my wife and children were similarly pigmented, this would be the kind of accommodation I would have to offer them.

And I had to ask myself that key question: Was I being judged by my quality as a human individual, or were people looking at me, seeing this visual mark of pigment and drawing up an indictment against a whole people?

The same held true in my search for employment. It is

clear that a person's ability to earn a livelihood in a decent manner is critical to his or her ability to live with any sense of dignity and self-respect.

The best jobs I got were menial—shining shoes, unloading trucks, carrying bags in a bus station. The most I ever earned in one day was $3.95. Since I tried to live on my earnings and since my room usually cost $3.00, little was left for food and transportation. I was reduced to eating beans and rice, or beans and pigtails, or beans and neckbones, but always beans. One day walking down a street I was astonished to hear myself spontaneously mutter, "Give us this day our daily beans."

In looking for employment I would usually study the help-wanted ads in the newspaper of any town I visited. Then I would telephone in answer to those ads. I would say exactly the truth: "This is John Griffin. I have just arrived in town and seen your ad." Then I would list the qualifications that made me feel I could do the job. I did not seek unrealistically ambitious employment. In those days, that would have been a waste of time. I answered ads, for example, for typists. I am a competent typist. One ad wanted a darkroom assistant in a photographic laboratory. I have had my own darkrooms for thirty years. I could do that kind of work.

In two cases I was simply too late and the jobs had already been filled. In every other instance my qualifications were good enough for the employer to ask me to come in for an interview or to fill out an application. Twice I was hired on the telephone and told to come on to work. But each time I appeared and it was seen that I was pigmented, I was immediately made to understand that I could not have those jobs.

There was no question but what this same man with the same name and exactly the same qualifications had a good portion of those jobs so long as they thought they were talking to a white man. The moment they saw I was black, even though I was the same man with the same name and the same qualifications, I could not get those jobs.

This kind of frustration has happened to the majority of black adults and often still does. Although it is now unlawful to discriminate in hiring practices, such discrimination remains massive. This is proved by statistics. In 1975, this country had a national unemployment figure of 7.9 percent, but one out of every four employable blacks was unemployed—25 percent. For every 100 black children under 18, 42.7 lived in poverty in 1975, whereas for every 100 white children under 18, only 14.9 lived in poverty. And the gap in median income between black and white families has actually *widened* in the ten years between 1965 and 1975. In 1965 the average black family had $59 in purchasing power for every $100 available to the white family; in 1975 it was $57.

These figures spring directly from inequities in employment and indirectly from discrimination in education. Whether directly or indirectly, they tell black Americans and other minority groups that racial discrimination remains massive and cruel even though we would like to think otherwise.

Recently I received a letter from a European firm expressing puzzlement and asking my advice about a job application they had received from a black American. The applicant, a man in his forties, held a masters degree in Romance languages. When asked to list his previous employment, he had carefully noted every job he had held. His list ran to three typewritten pages, and all except the last few had been menial jobs—custodian, busboy, service-station attendant, laborer. His potential European employers asked me if this made any sense. Why would a man with an academic degree hold so many jobs inappropriate to his education? I wrote them that, alas, it was perfectly understandable and that many distinguished black men and women of his generation had been obliged to hold such jobs in order to earn any kind of livelihood.

For seven weeks I traveled through the states of Louisiana, Mississippi, Alabama and Georgia. Toward the end of my experiment, each time I went to see a potential employer, I found myself internally pleading with him to do just one thing. I was not pleading for him to give me that job. No, I was begging him to ask me a question, just one question, and then reject me on the basis of my answer, not on the basis of my skin color.

When none did, I began to do something that many other black people were doing in those days. I stopped making those calls. I stopped looking for any kind of decent employment. What was the use? I stopped knocking on those doors because I finally understood that it doesn't matter who you are or what you can do as long as people insist on judging you by your color.

Whites talked about the problems of blacks as though such burdens sprang from blackness, from the color of a person's skin. But for black people, the burdens come not from blackness but from white people's seeming inability to see beyond that color to the human individual within.

So, I would look for places where I could simply sit and wait for the time to pass and blank my mind, because when you have a problem with no visible solution, it becomes unbearable even to think about it.

But one day when I was sitting on a door stoop in Alabama waiting for the hours to pass, an event occurred that made me realize that the sight of this black man sitting, waiting, was an injustice to all blacks because it reinforced the whites' stereotype of us. This realization came when I happened to glance up and see three white men dressed in business suits some distance away. One of them looked at me for a moment. I am not at all sure he saw me, though I felt that for the briefest instant we gazed squarely in each other's eyes. He then turned back to talk with the other men. That exchange of glances turned my consciousness from myself to him, and I saw myself suddenly as I must appear in the eyes of whites. What picture did I present to them? They saw a large, apparently strong black man, not badly dressed, idling there in the sunlight.

And I heard in my mind all the things whites might say under such circumstances.

"Look at that," one of them probably remarked. "Did you ever see such apathy? No wonder they can't get anywhere. If they'd just work and struggle and lift themselves up by their bootstraps ... get themselves an education. . . ."

"Well, I'll tell you one thing," another probably said. "If I was a big strong buck like that, I'd do *something.*

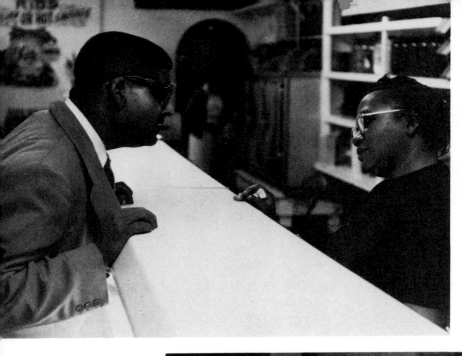

I'd dig ditches, anything. I wouldn't just sit there. . . ."

"No, they'd rather just sit there and do nothing and eat up our tax dollars in welfare funds. . . ."

It burned me to imagine what they were saying, because I have said the same things myself and I have grown up hearing white people saying them. Even the language takes on a different meaning in such circumstances. The word "apathy," for example. I thought of the games we played as children in which we had to hold our hands behind our backs and try to bite at an apple tied to a string. Every time we bit, someone would jerk the apple away. After a while we no longer bit at it. A stranger, not knowing what had gone on in the game, might come in and see the child just sitting there and conclude that the child was half dead from "apathy." Apathy was not the right word to use in the case of that child. Apathy was not the right word to use for us. It is not apathy when you have knocked on every door and been frustrated consistently.

And that other phrase by which whites told us that all we had to do was work, struggle, lift ourselves up by our bootstraps, get ourselves an education. How often we heard that admonition. It did not come from the overt bigot but from the sincere and concerned white. Do whites have any idea how such phrases sound to black people? What black people know to the marrow of their bones is that when whites discriminate against others on the basis of color, it does not matter in the slightest how much black people have worked, struggled, lifted themselves up by their bootstraps, or how many degrees they might hold.

Once in Alabama I went until 8:30 at night before I found a place where a black could get breakfast. No one ever asked me if I had academic degrees, or indeed any education at all, or if I had ever lifted myself up by my bootstraps. If I had been accompanied by every black college president in the country, I am sure all of us would have waited until 8:30 at night before we were served breakfast.

When I began my experiment, I believed like many whites that black people led essentially the same kind of lives we whites know, with certain inconveniences caused by discrimination and prejudice. But that is only the surface of a much deeper picture. The important thing is what racism does to a person's mind, concepts and whole way of functioning.

My deepest personal shock came with the gradual realization that this was not a matter of "inconvenience" but rather a matter of total change in living. Everything is different. Everything changes.

The first of these great changes occurred when I left the black hotel and went out into the community that first morning. As soon as I got into areas where I had contact with white people I realized that I was no longer regarded as a human individual. In our experience as whites, whenever we meet a stranger, an aura of mystery exists between us until the stranger discovers what kind of person we are and until we discover what kind of person that stranger is.

When a person is imprisoned in the stereotype others hold of him, that aura of mystery is wiped away. All of white society looked at black people, saw the pigment, and immediately attributed to us all the characteristics of the stereotype.

Surely one of the strangest experiences a person can have is suddenly to step out into the streets and find that the entire white society is convinced that individual possesses qualities and characteristics which that person knows he does *not* possess. I am not speaking here only of myself. This is the mind-twisting experience of every black person I know. Whites saw us and there was no mystery in us at all. They thought they knew everything about us. The sight of our black skin was all that whites required to know and judge us.

In their eyes we immediately were invested with certain "racial characteristics." They automatically assumed that we were indolent, irresponsible, had looser sexual morals, were apathetic, could not be trusted with money, probably had a violent streak; and also that we had a keen sense of humor, a God-given sense of rhythm, a good natural singing voice, a passion for watermelon and fried chicken. We were all of those things in the eyes of whites, though I never met a black person who considered himself in any way the embodiment of this bundle of qualities and characteristics.

Here whites will pounce on me and say: "You've never met a black who possesses all those characteristics. I can show you dozens who do."

Such whites say it the way they have seen it. I say it the way I have experienced it. And I think I can explain why they can say that and why I can say I never met a black who fit the stereotype insofar as authentic ethnic characteristics are concerned.

White people have always said, "We'll treat black people right as long as they stay in their place." If you pinned whites down, most could not say what that "place" is, but every black person knows—it is squarely in the middle of the stereotype. Whites created the stereotype to justify their racism and then forced black people to act out the stereotype. The same thing holds true with all racists and all victims of racism everywhere.

Racists say, "Don't tell me I don't know Negroes. Why, I've talked with Negroes about everything under the sun. You can't offend a Negro. They've got no pride. They're all alike." They will go on to ask why, if the stereotype is so untrue, blacks did not repudiate it?

The answer is simple. We could not repudiate the stereotype because whites would not let us. If we did not play the stereotyped role forced on us, they branded us "uppity, smart-alecky, arrogant." And every black knew that every day of every week blacks lost jobs, got beaten up, driven out or railroaded into jail for nothing more than being considered "uppity."

We had to play the stereotype in order to survive. In the black world we called it "climbing our mountain of 'yesses' and grinning, grinning, grinning." When we went out to work, or to look for work, in the morning, we would say, "We've got to put on that white-man's mask and go out there grinning and yessing." If we did not, then that white person, no matter how good or kind, could turn sour and become a threat to our job or to our continued existence in the community.

The stereotype forced a whole system of behavior on us, and if we deviated even slightly we were in trouble. I recall once in Mississippi when I was working at some menial job under a middle-aged white boss, he began to grow irritable with me. I could not guess what I was doing to upset him. Finally he exploded furiously at me. "What's eating you anyway?" he shouted.

"Nothing, sir," I said.

"Well, what're you being so damned sullen about?"

"Nothing, sir," I mumbled, trying not to increase his irritation.

"Well, I'll tell you one thing," he threatened. "If you want to hold a job around here you'd better show us some teeth."

He meant that I should be grinning, and my failure to do so had outraged him. So, of course, I plastered a grin on my face. I had no choice if I wanted to hold that job or to get any other job in the area. Had I got the reputation as a "sullen nigger," no one would have hired me for any kind of work.

So, whether we were shining shoes or loading trucks in the South, or waiting tables in Chicago, or scrubbing floors in Boston, white America saw us grin. They saw us grin everywhere and told themselves and the world that we "liked it that way" and that we were "a naturally happy-go-lucky people." If strangers came into the South, local whites would point to us with our grinning and yessing as proof that whites "treated us good" and that "we wanted nothing better than to live on as we were." They would even call us over to help them prove their point.

"John, say hello to Mr. So-And-So from Philadelphia. Now, tell him the truth. Are you happy here?"

"Oh, yes, sir."

"We treat you good? Tell him the truth."

"Yes, sir, you sure do," we'd say with a big smile, avoiding the stranger's eyes.

"Anybody ever treated you bad in this place?"

"No, sir—you all treat us real nice."

He would dismiss us to go back to our work, having proven his point to the stranger from Philadelphia or Detroit or wherever.

We had lied and grinned and yessed, even though he had urged us to "tell the truth." If we had dared, no matter how courteously, express the slightest disagreement, or tried to explain what the truth was for us, we would have lost our jobs or worse.

Whites have sometimes argued that I felt this degradation more deeply than black people because it was new to me, whereas black people had known nothing else all their lives. This is utterly untrue. It burns any man, and no person ever gets so accustomed to it that it does not burn.

One evening on a street corner near the outskirts of McComb, Mississippi, I was talking with two older black men. We became aware of a group of whites beginning to gather in front of a drugstore across the street. I do not want to give the impression that all whites were threats to us. Nevertheless, in that area whenever we saw a group of whites gathering nearby, we would begin to move away quietly, to "evaporate" as we called it. They might be all right. The chances were good that they were perfectly all right, but if you were black in that land you did not take chances. So we began to move away. But we did not move

back into the shadows soon enough. We heard a young man call from across the street, "Hey, Uncle, come over here."

At first we played deaf and kept walking. The young man called again, insistently, "Hey, Uncle, I said come over here." So the eldest turned and angled across the street back toward them. When our companion got to the curb we heard the young man say loudly, "Tell these fellows whose *boy* you are."

We walked on, not looking back, but listening.

The old man had no choice. We heard him speak in a voice heavy with the sweetness of sarcasm, "Yes, sir, I'm yours. You know that. I surely am yours."

We listened, wondering what would come next. Our companion continued insisting that he was the white youth's "boy" far beyond what was necessary, grinding it in, groveling in it. This was his way of ridiculing his tormenters and thereby salvaging something of his dignity. He knew that we heard and understood, and that he could exaggerate to the point of absurdity without the whites' understanding that he was throwing it in their faces.

The young man finally said, "Okay . . . you can go," and dismissed him. We continued walking down the street toward the next street lamp, and we heard our companion's footsteps slowly close the gap behind us. When he got within whispering distance, we heard his cursing, his rage welling up out of him like vomit.

You never get used to such prejudice.

One of the most moving moments in the television coverage of the historic Selma march came when newsmen interviewed some of the local white housewives. The ladies looked troubled and hurt by the black protests. They said they could not understand. "This has always been a nice place to live. And we've always treated our colored people right. Why should they want to act like this?"

I had never been in Selma as a white man, but I had been there as a black, and long before the world heard about Selma it was a terrible word in the vocabulary of black people. I sat in front of the TV that day and heard myself saying to the white ladies on the screen, "How can you stand up there and lie like that?"

But then I realized they were not lying. From their point of view, Selma was a nice town. And from what they could see of yessing and grinning black people, they really thought black people "liked it that way."

Then as we watched, newsmen questioned a local black lady, asking her to comment on what the white ladies had said. This black lady showed courage in telling the truth because she risked reprisals from the whites. "Oh yes," she said, "they treat us right as long as we think, look, act, grin, and do exactly what they want us to. But if we don't, then we lose our jobs, we get beaten up, we get killed." And that was the other side of the truth.

Black people referred to these contradictories as the "System." The System told us what whites really thought of us. It told us what we must do and how we must act in order to survive. The System varies in its details in different localities. I had to learn the details of the System as I moved from one city or state to another. For example, in New Orleans, no black could ride in a taxicab driven by a white driver, but in Mississippi we could.

When people simply accept the details of their local System, as in the case of the white ladies in Selma, an extraordinary thing happens. A community can live with a perfect illusion that it is good, that it is kind, that it enjoys "wonderfully harmonious relations" with its minorities, and never see that even kindness can be cruel in its effects on the victims so long as the community does not repudiate the System itself.

This began to come clear to me in New Orleans when I went into a drugstore that I had frequented before as a white man. The young lady behind the cash register was one of those profoundly and naturally courteous human beings of the sort black people used to call a "good white." I went in and made my purchases, gratified to see that she handled me with the same courtesy she had shown me when I was a white man.

I would have gone and written a good account of this encounter, but I happened to have a physical need which led me to ask a question that revealed how even an act of kindness can be cruel in its effects under the System.

"Pardon me. I'm diabetic," I said truthfully. "Could you tell me where is the nearest place I could find water?"

This young lady showed immediate concern and tried to be helpful. She ignored a drinking fountain with its water tap three steps to her right, leaned across the counter and said, "Oh, yes, now let me think where that would be. I'll tell you what. If you'll go out that door, and you take a left, you go up to that big boulevard three blocks away, and you take a right and go—I guess about fourteen blocks. I believe you'll find a place." She smiled encouragingly, glad to be helpful.

I was sure that if anyone suggested to that young woman that there is something cruel in sending a human being in need of water seventeen blocks when water is available three steps away, she would have been crushed. She was sure she was doing a good and kind act.

I was certain, given the kind of person she was, that if I had asked, "Pardon me, I am ill. Would you give me a glass of water?" she would not have hesitated to give me water. But I didn't ask that. I asked, "Where is the nearest place I could find water?" And this young lady, formed by this System, and I don't hesitate to say limited and handicapped by this formation, saw only the obvious. Here was a black man. Where was the nearest place she could direct him for water?

The seventeen blocks is not important. That is physical and the mere physical inconvenience was never the important thing in such incidents. The important thing is that for a time she regarded me as a human individual and treated me accordingly. But then my request for water triggered the old formation and suddenly she saw me only as someone "different." The important thing is that I stood there, as any black would, feeling for a moment that I was a human individual in her eyes, and then had it slapped in my face that I was only "the other."

This kind of rejection is repeated countless times in one way or another in the lives of all minority people in a racist society. When it is sustained it creates resentments that burn deeply. These resentments were not turned so much against the overt bigot, because we did not have much to do with the overt bigot. No, they were turned against the good white people in the streets, people like the young woman in the drugstore. We would look at people whose faces radiated decency—at teachers, doctors, judges, ministers, priests, nuns—people who would never deliberately be unkind. And we would feel like shouting in their faces, "Do you know what you've got? Your mind is free to dwell on something better, something higher. But because you won't say no to this System, you are part of the giant white hand that keeps our minds crammed down into our bellies."

Of course we didn't do that. We knew that they would not, could not, have the slightest idea of what we were talking about.

s Brooklyn Bombing

O'Brien said the word on the street is that the bombs "Were a warning to Tyronne [Miss Viales' 18-year son]. They weren't after because he was black. T had a specific reason."

Last night Officer Rob Feldman of the station hou confirmed that McCur face assault charges for alteration he had with fo neighborhood. Blacks las

police were not aware the FBI had entered the case. McCurdy...

Blacks Attacked by Whi With Clubs in Washing

By JOSEPH B. TREASTER

A band of at least 20 white youths armed through Washington Square ling racial epithets

Sergeant quoted wit 200 person al-states...

Racially Mixed Family Harassed By White Youths in Pelham Bay

By JOSEPH B. TREASTER

Ten days ago Nicholas Troiano, who is white, and his wife, Louise, who is black, took possession of a $60,000 two-story frame house in the predominantly white Pelham Bay section of the Bronx.

And they haven't had a moment's peace since.

White youths have yelled racial sl at the newcomers, shot in the hous

He said that leads to the arrested youths were developed through witnesses to the early morning incident and added that he was particularly pleased that "we did get the co tion of the comm

Chicano's Death Stirs a Texas Region

behalf of blacks in the South had ignored similar injustices Americans.

tional facts in the Morales cas had come to Federal attentio The reversal came after G Briscoe. Senators Llo

By JAMES P. STERB
Special to The New York Time

CASTROVILLE, Tex., A — Eleven months ago, moon-lit gravel road fiv west of town, Frank the 52-year-old Castro lice Chief, put the bar sawed-off 12-gauge sho der the left armpit of Morales and pulled th of Mr. M

White Youths Terrorize Black Family in S.I. Home

By ROBERT D. McFADDEN

Two carloads of white youths armed with baseball bats, an ax, knives and tree limbs battered their way into a black

drawings from Mr. Warren's collection of about 100 works of art.

Inside the 10-foot-square

Discrimination Remains a

By PAUL DELANEY
Special to The New York Times

CHICAGO, Sept. 12—In suburban Washington, black-skinned members of the diplomatic corps can join the Chevy Chase Country Club, but not black American residents of the area, not even the black mayor of the na

than for blacks, Latins and now eligible for the Maids where an official of the club that four Jews were among year. They are eligible for Amagansett L.I. where one

FOUR

The reader will say, "But that is all in the past. They've taken down the old WHITE ONLY signs. It's no longer like that."

In a sense that is true. It is more convenient for black people to exist today because they do not have such problems taking care of fundamental physical needs. But the essential damage is still there and so is the repressive system in a new wrapping.

Today minority people can eat and sleep almost anywhere and can use unsegregated rest rooms. But deeper problems of discrimination in employment, housing, schooling, banking, business, health services, churches and courts remain massive and crippling. Such discrimination makes itself felt in thousands of subtle ways that the laws have not touched and probably cannot ever touch.

So minority people continue to bear the burdens of injustice which spring from a racism that goes largely uncorrected in most contemporary societies. In fact, since the early 1970s we have seen a resurgence of open, unashamed, brazen racism around the world.

Look at the purely racist resolution in the United Nations equating Zionism with racism. This is part of the growing anti-Semitism that spreads like a sickness as people forget where it led in Nazi Germany. Today in Milwaukee and Chicago the Jewish councils seek relief from the harrassment of local Nazis who have been demonstrating and distributing literature expressing hatred of black and Jewish people.

Look at the rise of anti-Semitism even among some black people. Look at the phenomenon of prejudice shown by some minority groups against other minority groups. As one group emerges from discrimination into acceptance, very often it becomes the worst discriminator against the group beneath, largely because its people do not want to be associated in the public's mind with people who represent their own past sufferings. For example, in areas where Chicano people are less discriminated against than blacks, some of them will have little to do with blacks for fear Chicanos will suffer greater repression.

Look at the rise in KKK activity by Klans that now openly advertise in newspapers—in New York State as well as in Louisiana. Do we take them seriously? The temptation is to dismiss them as ridiculous crackpots; but they create a climate of violent repression, and they have a history of torture and murder that leads right up to our days.

Look at the criminal injustices continuing against Native American Indians. These are unarguable, no one even denies them. Yet they continue in ways that outrage every decent instinct. Who has read in the newspapers about the lynchings near Farmington, New Mexico? Most news media simply ignore such things. In April 1974, the bodies of three Navajo men were found in separate locations in the canyons near Farmington. They had been beaten, tortured and burned.

The slaughter did not end there. In June 1975, Merle Burton, aged seventy, a Navajo, was assaulted and tortured. He died of severe internal injuries the next day after saying a white man had attacked him. In a bizarre perversion of justice, two FBI agents and a Bureau of Indian Affairs policeman arrested not a "white man" but Farmington's only albino Navajo. He was released when he proved he could not possibly have been involved. In that same summer of 1975, four other Navajos were murdered in the area. If you read ethnic and Native American newspapers such as *Akwesasne Notes*, you will see that these are only a few of the lynchings of Native Americans that occur in this land.

We tend to look on these moments of violent excess and view them as isolated "accidents." The bombing of the children in Birmingham; the murder of civil rights advocates like Medgar Evers, Clyde Kennard, Martin Luther King, Jr.; the Klan executions of Schwerner, Chaney and Goodman, of Vernon Dahmer and more recently of Reverend Pace: we hear these atrocities, but since they occur in different areas of the country and have no apparent connection, many have supposed they were spontaneous crimes, that racists' tempers flared and they killed. But this is not true. All these incidents required careful planning and execution.

These are not "accidents"—they are the products of generations of racism. As John Redhouse of the Navajo community commented after the canyon lynchings in New Mexico, "We didn't see the murders as the acts of three crazy kids—we saw it as part of a whole racist picture. For years it has been almost a sport, a sort of sick, perverted tradition among Anglo youth of Farmington High School to go into the Indian section of town and physically assault and rob elderly and sometimes intoxicated Navajo men and women of whatever possessions they had, for no apparent reason other than that they were Indians."

What kind of people and what kind of societies does racism produce? Let us look at one case in some detail because it is a classic example of how an entire community can be subverted.

I first met Vernon Dahmer when I went to Hattiesburg, Mississippi, to visit the mother of martyred Clyde Kennard, shortly after Kennard's death. Racial tensions were high in Mississippi. Violence was in the air. I talked with Kennard's mother on the telephone, telling her I had arrived in Hattiesburg and would like to come to her farm on the outskirts of town. She arranged for Mr. Dahmer to pick me up and drive me to her farm. In those days it took some bravery for a black man to drive a white stranger anywhere in that area. Vernon Dahmer, a local black leader, large and seemingly fearless, drove me to the meeting with Kennard's mother. He impressed me as a man of great seriousness. We did not talk much. He was taking me on an errand of mercy to help Kennard's elderly mother. He was such an impressive man I could not forget him.

The next time I heard of Vernon Dahmer, he had been murdered. Here is his story as I was able to reconstruct it with the help of local people in Hattiesburg and from court records.

Members of Klaverns 4 and 5 of the White Knights of the Ku Klux Klan in the Laurel-Hattiesburg area of Mississippi had been watching Vernon Dahmer for a long time. In December 1965, the "Dahmer Project," as it was called by local Klansmen, became a matter of urgent business when Dahmer outraged whites by collecting poll taxes in his store for black people who were too frightened to pay them at the sheriff's office.

At the Klan meeting in Jones County, someone brought up the subject of the Dahmer Project. The matter was quickly hushed up, and those present were told they would have to wait for orders from Imperial Wizard Sam Bowers, Jr.

A subsequent meeting in Laurel was held in an old barn on the farm of Lawrence Bird with Imperial Wizard Bowers present and in a rage over Dahmer's activities in registering black voters at his store five miles outside of Hattiesburg, south of Laurel. Bowers pounded on the table and shouted that something had to be done "about that damned nigger down south." He said they were long overdue in "handling" Dahmer.

Careful plans were made in that December meeting. They decided the "Dahmer job" should be a No. 3 project and also a No. 4 project. In Klan talk, a No. 3 project meant arson and a No. 4 project meant "abolishment, death." (No. 1 meant harrassment, No. 2 meant a beating.) So the verdict called for Vernon Dahmer to be burned out and killed.

A few days later, men from Klaverns 4 and 5 made what they called a "dry run." During this rehearsal, they drove past Vernon Dahmer's home and store and made highly detailed final plans. They would strike both home and store simultaneously and each man would be assigned a specific task to perform.

They chose a brilliant, cold moonlit night because part of their plan called for them to drive away from the scene without headlights. Shortly after midnight on January 10, 1966, Klansmen met at a service station, filled some plastic jugs with gasoline, and set out in two cars toward the Dahmer property some twenty miles to the south.

Inside the brick and wood home, Vernon Dahmer and his wife and children were asleep. Dahmer knew he lived under constant threat, so he slept with two shotguns and two pistols beside his bed.

When the two carloads of Klansmen arrived in front of the Dahmer home, they saw that the house was completely dark. They moved rapidly. Two of the men began firing, having been ordered to shoot out the front-room windows so the jugs of gasoline could be thrown inside. Another, Charles Clifford Wilson, hurried around to the carport to set fire to Dahmer's car and pickup truck.

According to the later testimony of Billy Roy Pitts, he and Cecil Sessum, a part-time minister called "Little Preacher," ran to the house and squatted down at the brick front. Little Preacher Sessum stabbed holes in five of the plastic jugs and tossed them through the window into the house. He used two or three matches to light a torch he had made from a forked stick wrapped in gasoline soaked rags. He threw it inside where gasoline had leaked from the containers.

One of Dahmer's neighbors, J. B. Smith, getting ready to go deer hunting, saw the brightness of a moonlit sky suddenly glow red in the direction of Dahmer's place, but supposed Dahmer was burning off the slag pile from his small sawmill.

A blaring car horn awakened Mrs. Dahmer. The car in their carport was on fire and the blaze had short-circuited the horn. She shook her husband awake, shouting above the roar of the fire. Smoke fumes spread to the sleeping quarters, choking the family as they ran to the back to attempt an escape through one of the windows.

In front, Billy Roy Pitts thought he heard a man's voice from inside.

"Let him die," Little Preacher Sessum told him as they rushed back to their cars.

Mrs. Dahmer attempted to lift her ten-year-old daughter, Betty, out of the window, but she lost her balance and fell out herself. She heard a continuous fusillade of shots being fired into the house. Her husband had turned back and was returning the gunfire from inside. When she shouted, he hurried back and handed Betty through the window to her mother. Dennis, their twelve-year-old son, climbed out the window, but returned inside when they realized that an older son, Harold, had not been awakened by the noise. Dennis dashed into the smoke and shook his brother awake. Vernon Dahmer smashed out the window framing with the butt of his shotgun and escaped the blazing house with his two sons.

The Klansmen got into their cars and quickly drove away. The driver of the second car forgot the orders to drive a long distance without headlights. Men from the other car fired their guns, hoping to shoot out the lights. Their bullets blew the tires. Their orders were to burn up the car if anything went wrong, but since they had no gasoline left they had to abandon it. It served later as evidence in their trial. All of the men crowded into the remaining car and drove toward Laurel.

The Dahmers huddled in their barn. Their son, Harold, dashed into the blazing carport and managed to back out the pickup truck before it was too damaged by fire. He drove to the home of a relative to call the fire department. When he returned, he loaded the family into the pickup and started toward town. On the road they met Dahmer's sister, Mrs. Earline Beard, who had come to help. She transferred them to her car and took them to Forrest General Hospital.

J. B. Smith checked his deer-hunting gear, climbed into his car, and headed out the driveway. As he was about to enter the road, a single car going north passed in front of his headlights. He heard men laughing and talking and thought he recognized one of them as Cecil Sessum, Little Preacher, whom he had known for several years.

At the hospital, the Dahmers were examined for injuries. Mrs. Dahmer was burned on the arm. Both of Betty's arms were burned. Vernon Dahmer, still dressed in pajama shirt and undershorts, suffered burns on both arms. His face was covered with soot, but his wife saw no other burns on him.

The carload of Klansmen arrived at Little Preacher Sessum's home shortly after 3:00 A.M. and prepared quietly to disperse. Before they left, Sessum, who was Exalted Cyclops of the Jones County Klavern No. 4, warned the men not to talk. He said that if anyone did talk about the events of that night, he would find himself in a barrel of cement.

By early morning, Vernon Dahmer was in great pain. He was given Demerol shots for the pain of his external and internal burns, and Seconal to help him rest. At 1:30 in the afternoon of that same January 10, Mrs. Dahmer went in to see him and said "he looked to be resting well."

In early midafternoon Vernon Dahmer raised up in bed and called out for his wife. He was struggling for breath. The nurses came in and worked desperately, but within twenty minutes he was dead. Two pathologists, Dr. Thomas F. Puckett and Dr. Robert Cooke, performed an autopsy which revealed that the bronchial tubes had been scorched when Dahmer breathed the hot fumes inside his house, and this had been the cause of death.

Although their No. 3 Project (arson) and No. 4 Project (death) had been successfully completed, the night raiders had in the words of Little Preacher Sessum, "Really loused up that job." The efforts of the prosecutors were immensely aided when Billy Roy Pitts decided to turn state's evidence, confessed all the details of the crime, and named everyone involved. Pitts, closely guarded as the state's chief witness in the long series of trials that followed, received a five-year sentence for complicity in depriving Vernon Dahmer of his civil rights, and a mandatory life sentence for his part in the murder—a sentence he has never been brought in to serve. In trials held in 1968 and 1969, some of the participants received life sentences, some lesser sentences, and some were freed in mistrials. Cecil Sessum and Charles Clifford Wilson were given life sentences.

A special interest attaches to Charles Clifford Wilson, who drove one of the cars, fired into the house, and set fire to the Dahmer's car and carport. Wilson, thirty-four at the time of the assassination, was county investigator for the White Knights of the KKK and a member of Klavern No. 5. This strange, seemingly gentle man was highly respected in Laurel where he operated the Laurel Brace and Limb Company. The Laurel Junior Chamber of Commerce gave him their *Man of the Year Distinguished Service Award* just three days before he was indicted for murder and arson. A number of the character witnesses at his trial spoke of his work in aiding crippled and retarded children.

Wilson and some of the other defendants were held in such high esteem by local white citizens that on March 9, 1968, a fund-raising dinner was held at the Pinehurst Hotel in Laurel to raise money for their defense. The affair was publicized in both the Laurel and Hattiesburg newspapers, and a crowd of some three hundred paid $10 each to eat fried chicken and hear speakers. Tickets for the event read: "Proceeds to defend our white Christian citizens being charged and persecuted under the so-called Civil Rights Acts." The dinner chairman, Mrs. Sybil Nix, reported to the media that the dinner was a "big success" and stated that "white Christian American patriots are beginning to organize themselves politically for the first time in years."

What kind of a society does racism produce? Obviously a society in which arson and murder are perfectly acceptable ingredients in the makeup of "Christian American patriots."

Charles Clifford Wilson appealed his conviction and his

life sentence, engaging attorney William L. Waller to handle the legal aspects of the appeal. His appeal was unsuccessful, and in 1969 Wilson entered Parchman, the state penitentiary, to begin serving his life sentence.

On December 23, 1972, after Wilson had served a scant three years of his life sentence, the governor of Mississippi announced he had released Wilson from the penitentiary under a recently inaugurated "work-release" program. Interestingly, the new governor was William L. Waller, Wilson's unsuccessful appeals lawyer. Wilson was assigned to the Southern Mississippi State Hospital in his hometown of Laurel. He lives at home with his wife and children and also has time to run the Laurel Brace and Limb Company.

The announcement caused shock and anger among many blacks and some whites in Mississippi. The shock and anger deepened when it was revealed that Wilson, in the preceding three years, had been allowed to go home on leave eight times, some of these leaves granted by Governor Waller and others by former Governor John Bell Williams. These "special leaves" had varied in length from forty-eight hours to three months. Waller had granted him two ninety-day leaves in 1973—all of this before the new and legally dubious work-release program was instituted.

A white state senator from Corinth, Theodore Smith, called the governor's action "illegal as hell," explaining that the legislature had refused to pass the bill establishing this kind of program.

When challenged about the illegality of his actions, the governor said he had granted the special leaves and now the work-release because Wilson's wife and children needed him at home—a claim almost any prisoner with dependents could make. Waller also justified his actions on the grounds that Wilson's work with braces and artificial limbs was needed in Laurel.

Vernon Dahmer's widow, speaking of Wilson's family, said, "Of course, if their father and husband is living, they have more to look to than we have. All we have out there is a tombstone and a grave." Wilson's release, she felt, would do nothing but encourage Klansmen, "and we have to live here with fear. How can we ever forget a night like January 10th?"

Blacks and whites have joined Mrs. Dahmer's protests and have accused the governor of giving violent white racists "a license to kill black citizens."

Recalling the fact that the governor was formerly Wilson's appeals attorney, Mrs. Dahmer said, "He has now done as governor what he was not able to do as Wilson's lawyer."

Is this very special treatment of a convicted murderer really a move in the direction of more enlightened handling of prisoners, a first step in much-needed prison reform, as Governor Waller contends? If so, it is odd that Waller picked a former client as one of the first beneficiaries. Waller has been accused of making the first move toward fulfilling private election promises to white racists. He denies this.

The Delta-Democrat Times in Greenville editorialized: "If Wilson were black, had murdered or raped a white woman and were released so often and so casually by state authorities, the outcry would be deafening. But Wilson is white, his victim was black and his lawyer is now the Governor of Mississippi. The protests are few and far between from white Mississippians."

Once, in Louisiana, I got a close look from the "inside" of what Klansmen really believed. I was on an investigative trip when my car battery went dead in Ferriday, Louisiana, near the Mississippi border. I sought help from a local filling station and they brought my car in to recharge the battery. I realized I was in hostile territory—hostile to me and my ideas at least—when the proprietor of the station asked me if I had any explosives in my car. I told him I did not. He said, "I thought maybe you were headed into Mississippi to blow up some of those outside agitators," meaning the civil rights workers who were there registering black voters. "And I thought if you were, I'd give you the battery recharge free."

"Not this time," I said, setting my camera case down on the counter.

He glanced curiously at my case and noticed my name on the cover.

"Are you John Griffin?" he asked, as though astonished.

"I suppose I am," I mumbled, expecting him to throw me out, or worse.

"Well, let me shake your hand," he beamed excitedly. I realized he was mistaking me for the John Griffin who was a famous Klan leader in Alabama and who had been serving a prison sentence for having helped a fellow Klansman castrate a young black man.

I was sure of the mistake when he called in his assistant and told him to "come in here and shake hands with John Griffin from Alabama."

Confused by the mistake, I shook hands and accepted the warmth and cordiality with which they surrounded me. This station, they explained, was the local Klan headquarters. They even had a Klan mailbox behind the counter.

By mistake I had penetrated the Klan, and I could not very well admit my real identity. I was on the Klan Bureau of Investigation's hate lists.

They spread the word that I was in town. Other Klansmen began to show up at the station, with broad smiles and warm handshakes. In the summer heat of early afternoon we visited under the shade of the station roof.

I kept as quiet as possible while they questioned me about their plans. One of the older men said in a tone of great sadness, "If we'd all stood firm behind Governor Faubus during the ruckus in Little Rock, we wouldn't have to be fighting our separate battles today."

Another said, "We've got some good people here, Griffin. We haven't given up yet." They then asked my opinion about a plan of theirs—to meet at the gas station some morning around one or two when everyone would be asleep in "niggertown." They would each take five-gallon cans of gasoline and burn up all the wooden shanties. They spoke of killing "every man, woman and child—get rid of all of them."

I told them that if they did such a thing they would mess up our "national plans," and that they had better wait for the right moment.

"And we're going to get all those damned white preachers, too," one of them promised.

"What have they been up to?" I asked.

"Well, you know about St. Peter—how he could walk on the water as long as he kept his mind fixed on Jesus? But when he took his mind off of Jesus, he sank. Well, that's the way with these preachers. They were all right as long as they kept their minds fixed on Jesus. But they've taken their minds off of Jesus and started talking this 'brotherhood' stuff, and we're going to get rid of them."

"That's right," another nodded soberly. "If they can't keep their minds on Jesus, let 'em sink."

I realized these were serious men, deeply sincere in their desires to keep the old ways at whatever cost in human lives and misery. I was shaken to perceive that these men were as sincerely generous in their love for me, thinking me a fellow Klansman, as they would be merciless to me if they knew who I really was.

It would be a grave mistake to think that such racist poisoning is regional, that it exists only in the South, or that it is directed only against black people. It exists in every corner of the world where racist elements can dominate decent men and women and manipulate decent societies. It exists wherever men look on fellow human beings as "intrinsically other" and do not say no at the very first sign of racist injustice.

Another of Burke's statements applies here: "All that is required for the triumph of evil," he said, "is simply that good men remain silent long enough."

This was certainly true in Nazi Germany. With rare and magnificent exceptions, academic, civic, professional and religious leadership equivocated. One heard them say things that might be translated into English as "Let's not rock the boat," and "Let's not disturb the peace," even though the peace to which they referred was a kind of negative peace based on inaction in the presence of great injustice—and therefore always an explosive "peace." These are exactly the same things people say in this country in criticism of civil-rights martyrs—"If they had minded their own business, they wouldn't have got killed." The silence of good men. . . .

FIVE

On my journey as a black man through the South, I noticed a subtle change in the general atmosphere when I arrived in Montgomery, Alabama. Although black people lived in fear and under nearly total suppression, the underlying despair and sense of helplessness were less evident.

Four years earlier, on December 1, 1955, the modern civil rights movement had begun in Montgomery. Black people had proved a point—at least to themselves: something could be done if people were sufficiently determined and if they stuck together regardless of reprisals.

Montgomery was already festooned with Christmas decorations when Mrs. Rosa Parks, an attractive young seamstress, walked to a corner bus stop downtown and boarded the Cleveland Avenue bus.

She walked to the back of the bus, to the section marked COLORED and sat in the first row of seats behind the sign. As the bus filled and white patrons had no more room, the bus driver ordered the four black patrons seated on the first row behind the sign to vacate their seats so the whites could have them. It was traditional. No black person could be seated while a white had to stand. The other three blacks in the front row immediately obeyed. Mrs. Parks hesitated. She saw that every seat in the "colored" section was occupied. If she complied she would have to stand while a white man took the seat for which she had paid. She quietly refused to move. She was tired and her feet were sore. She was tired in other ways, too: tired of being forever second class, tired of being battered by the System.

The bus driver had her arrested. She was jailed on a charge of disobeying the city segregation ordinance.

Ordinarily this would have been just another incident. "Trouble makers" occasionally surfaced from the black community. Severe punishment usually restored order.

This time, it did not. The black community in Montgomery was a powder keg of accumulated resentments from past slappings, cursings and unjust arrests. This small incident caused it to explode into massive protest over Mrs. Parks's arrest. The young seamstress had unknowingly touched off a revolution that was to catapult a local minister, Martin Luther King, Jr., twenty-seven, from obscurity to world prominence.

Early the next morning, Friday, December 2, black civic leader E. D. Nixon telephoned Dr. King. "We have taken this type of thing too long already," he said. "I feel the time has come to boycott the buses. Only through a boycott can we make it clear to the white folks that we will not accept this type of treatment any longer."

Since the largest part of the bus company's passengers were black people, a boycott could be effective. But would it work? King feared the people would be too vulnerable to reprisals.

During the weekend, as many black people as possible were contacted. In churches, ministers announced the message. "We can no longer lend our cooperation to an evil system." Mimeographed leaflets were distributed throughout the community. The news spread.

On Monday morning the Kings were up at five o'clock. A bus stop only a few feet from their house made it convenient for them to watch from their window. The first bus would pass at 6:00 A.M. Dr. King felt that if they could get sixty-percent cooperation in the boycott, the protest would be a success.

The six o'clock bus passed. It was empty. The South Jackson line, which passed their house, was usually jammed with domestic workers going to their jobs. A second bus passed—empty. A third bus contained only two passengers, both of them white. Instead of the sixty-percent cooperation they had hoped for, it became apparent they had almost one hundred percent.

Buses drove about empty, with motorcycle police as escorts. Blacks walked or hitched rides to work. Unconventional transportation was seen. Men rode mules to work. Others used horse-drawn buggies. Most walked. The atmosphere turned festive. Blacks began to cheer the empty buses. Children sang out, "No riders today."

Martin Luther King preached nonviolent resistance in a way that captured the imagination of blacks and whites alike. He compared their protest to methods used by the Klans and White Citizens Councils. "Their methods lead to violence and lawlessness," he said. "But in our protest there will be no cross burnings. No white person will be taken from his home by a hooded Negro mob and brutally murdered. There will be no threats and intimidation."

Under the leadership of Dr. King and his colleagues in Montgomery, black people discovered the weapon of nonviolent resistance and were transformed from a cowed and resentful people into a united, fearless community. They walked for freedom, day after day, month after month. One elderly woman summed up the whole spirit of the movement. Asked if she were tired, she said, "My feets is tired, but my soul is at rest."

The "official" white community, including the police and civic officials, struck back, carrying out a program of harassment and reprisals against blacks. But most of their strategy backfired, because black people had changed. They were no longer afraid. They no longer considered it a disgrace to go to jail. They accepted the blows, curses, hate stares as marks of honor. Blacks who took the beatings, then knelt and prayed for those who beat them.

Typical of this change is an incident involving the Ku Klux Klan. The Klan decided to stop the "foolishness" by putting on their white sheets and marching through the ghetto. Always before when the Klan had marched, blacks had cleared the streets and hidden in their homes. But this time they rushed out of their homes, lined the sidewalks, waved and cheered as they would at any parade. A sinister demonstration was turned into a festivity. The Klan made no more marches.

The groundwork for nonviolent resistance had been laid in Montgomery. In the early 1960s, a great many Americans of all ethnic groups awakened to the gravity of racial prejudice and discrimination and rose up to demand that this country live up to its promises to all of its citizens.

Black people, usually joined by whites, began to "sit-in" at segregated lunch counters, refusing to leave even though they would not be served. They behaved in orderly fashion but they were often arrested and hauled off to jail.

Marches, boycotts and other nonviolent techniques grew more frequent.

This was a time of hope for black and white Americans alike. Ardent racists were beginning to be viewed as sick and severely handicapped people, rather than as patriots. This realization led more and more people into nonviolent resistance. Everywhere people were saying, "It's going to be up to us to save racists from their racism."

The principle of nonviolent resistance challenged black people to love their oppressors until those oppressors were cured of the terrible sickness of racism, healed, and liberated from the need to oppress others. At the same time it called for firm resistance to the injustices of racism.

If a person drifted toward hate, he was warned. "Don't let them make you hate. If they can make us hate, then they will have won." Advocates of nonviolent resistance believed, prophetically, that only the racist would benefit if hatred were hurled against hatred.

In those early years of 1960, many Americans believed in this new vision; they marched, they prayed, they sacrificed, they sang, they took the beatings and the spittings and the cattle prods and the jailings and went on praying for their abusers—those racists who called themselves Christians and patriots.

Despite all of the difficulties and setbacks, hopes were high because more and more white people were willing to suffer the consequences and "put their bodies where their mouths were" in standing beside blacks for what we professed to believe. Whites died, went to jail, were beaten alongside blacks.

Until the 1960s, this country suffered from two massive

delusions. The first was the delusion of Southern whites that they alone knew and understood black people, that no outsider could possibly understand the situation, and that black people "liked it that way." I never in my life met a black person who "liked it that way" or who felt any Southern white understood anything about black people.

The other delusion, widely held in all areas of this country, was simply that "it was not like that here."

In the 1960s, both delusions were shattered, to the bewilderment of whites everywhere. People all over this land began to realize that it was "like that" in their ghettos, that black people suffered essentially the same problems everywhere. And Southern whites learned, through the demonstrations, that black people did not "like it that way." Nevertheless, these delusions still remain with many people.

Largely as a result of the great ferment, the demonstrations and the martyrdom of so many civil rights advocates, a civil rights bill was passed in 1964 which reaffirmed the rights and liberties of citizens as guaranteed in the Constitution. This immediately made illegal many local discriminatory ordinances that had been passed in various states. It outlawed discrimination in all public places and in employment and education, and guaranteed voter registration rights.

But despite massive efforts to make this country live up to its promise of equal justice and equal opportunities for all, prejudice and discrimination continued to plague minority people, as it does to this day. The prejudiced simply found ways to get around the civil rights laws.

As a result of this kind of cheating, this country has

gone from good solutions to poor solutions in many instances. For example, in the matter of equal employment opportunities, at first blacks said, "We do not want any black person employed on a token basis, as window dressing. We do not want any white deprived of a job to make a job for a black. On the other hand, we do not want blacks held back from jobs or promotions just because they are black." No one could ask for a higher ethical solution than that.

When it was clear that this proposal was not being met in good faith by white employers, other solutions were proposed. When those were not met in good faith, then admittedly-poor solutions were advanced. As a last resort, a quota system was enforced as a way of insuring against discrimination in employment. This was seen as a regrettable solution by blacks as well as by whites. It was adopted only because the good solutions were not met in good faith.

Blacks, of course, would still prefer to have people employed on the basis of their job qualifications, but until people set aside prejudice in employment, the quota system will be necessary to insure that the law is not subverted. Blacks still prefer the good solutions, while accepting the poorer solutions as the only way to achieve justice and equality *at this time.*

The same picture holds true for busing. Because people offered so much resistance to open housing, keeping black people from moving into homes in "white areas," neighborhood schools were segregated. No one objected when buses were used to carry children to segregated schools. It was only when it came to busing children to desegregated schools that the public began to protest. Had we not cheated massively in the issue of open housing, neighborhoods would be desegregated and so would the neighborhood schools, and busing would not be needed to achieve racial balance in the schools.

After the 1964 civil rights bill failed to eliminate massive discrimination, black people began to believe that all the marching, all the praying, all the forgiving, all the unearned suffering were not going to accomplish the dream after all. Nonviolent resistance came to be viewed as a failure. In frustration and bitterness, black people came to the conclusion that most whites were too deeply entrenched in their racism ever to change.

Whites, even very sincere white leaders in the cities, had little knowledge of conditions in the ghettos of their own cities. Black reactions to racial incidents became more abrasive. White leaders began to call me into the cities, to live in the ghettos and then consult with them about the real sources of unrest in these inner cities. I was called into Rochester (New York), into Watts, into Detroit, Cleveland, St. Louis, Wichita and others.

My long stays in the inner cities convinced me again that this was a land with two groups of people possessing two entirely different sets of information and experience: the majority whites and the minority peoples. The majority did not know, had no idea, what was going on in the minority communities. They viewed everything from outside and from their own perspective.

In each of these cities, I lived with black people and then I came out and gave the same warnings. I said the inner cities were hellholes of frustration and hopelessness, that people felt imprisoned within the invisible boundaries of the ghettos, and that they could only judge whites from the evidence presented to them. That evidence suggested they were caught in a trap of injustice. They paid higher prices for second-rate goods, they lived in buildings owned by absentee white landlords who rarely made any improvements. They were frequently subject to inept and rude police handling, so that they came to view the police not as their protectors but as their abusers. I warned that tensions and despair were at the breaking point. I said they were like powder kegs and we were like children tossing matches at them. One day, one of those matches would detonate the powder kegs and we would be astonished to see such a massive explosion over such a seemingly insignificant provocation.

In each city, the community leaders, those who lived there and thought they knew their areas, felt that I was being "unduly pessimistic," yet all of those cities exploded in what came to be known as the "riots." In every case, some seemingly minor incident caused the inner cities to explode.

The explosions usually followed a similar pattern: A rumor would be started, sometimes by telephone to a city official, stating that a nearby city was in flames and that carloads of armed blacks were headed to the neighboring city to destroy it. Wichita, Kansas, received that message, saying Kansas City was in flames and blacks were coming. Cedar Rapids, Iowa, received that call saying Des Moines was in flames. Ardmore, Oklahoma, received that call saying Oklahoma City was in flames. Reno, Nevada, received that call saying Oakland was in flames. Norfolk, Virginia, received that call saying Richmond was in flames. The list could go on and on. None of these cities was in flames. No carloads of armed black people ever showed up to destroy the threatened cities.

But the calls created a climate of panic. White leadership was notified. Riot control measures were put into effect. White civilians armed themselves. The communities became armed camps, waiting for the black attack. Again, in all of these communities, black people were generally unaware of what was going on. Since most of the incidents occurred at night, most blacks were in their homes. Some did occur in daylight hours. In Fresno, California, an alarm was spread one Saturday morning. A white businessman was notified. He called a young black teacher of his acquaintance and told him of the report that the black community was going to "riot."

"I haven't heard anything about it," the young black teacher said.

The white businessman asked him to look around the neighborhood and see if anything looked suspicious. The teacher did and returned to the phone.

"It's pretty ominous, I'm afraid," he said with mock seriousness. "There's a man across the street mowing his lawn, and down on the corner I saw a woman out walking with her little girl. You'd better take precautions."

But most often, no black was notified or consulted. Whites armed themselves and waited for the explosion. In such an atmosphere, any kind of incident could set it off. In Wichita, after such preparations had been made against the alleged carloads of armed blacks coming in from Kansas City, five white youths drove into the black area and shot off their guns. Blacks came out of their houses and, seeing what happened, threw rocks and sticks at the carload of white youths. A near riot was on. Police apprehended the five white youths and twelve young blacks. They judged that the most outraged of the young blacks, a college student who held two jobs to pay for his education, was the "leader" of the stone-throwing blacks. They put him in a separate police car to take him to jail. He was intact when he got into the car. When they arrived at jail, he had been badly beaten and lacerated and had a broken arm.

The five whites and twelve blacks spent the night in jail. The next day the five whites, all of whom had been arrested bearing arms, were released on bonds of $1,000 each. The twelve blacks, none of whom was armed, were released on bonds of $5,000 each. Blacks waited for whites to protest this inequity in bonding. To be an unarmed black was to be penalized five times as heavily as an armed white. When not a single white seemed to see anything wrong with it, black people began to hold "rage meetings." This was an open injustice, an open inequity. It is by such things that black people judge the intentions of whites.

I was asked to attend one of the rage meetings in Wichita. The young men, including the physically abused college student, were present. Their parents and neighbors and ministers were there.

A few of the young men spoke, their talks full of passion, their words interrupted with "Amens" from the crowd. I said nothing; I listened. At a previous meeting an older, burned-out black man had said I would be welcome to talk, but he had warned, "Don't say any-